COOL CARS

MCLAREN

ARTURA

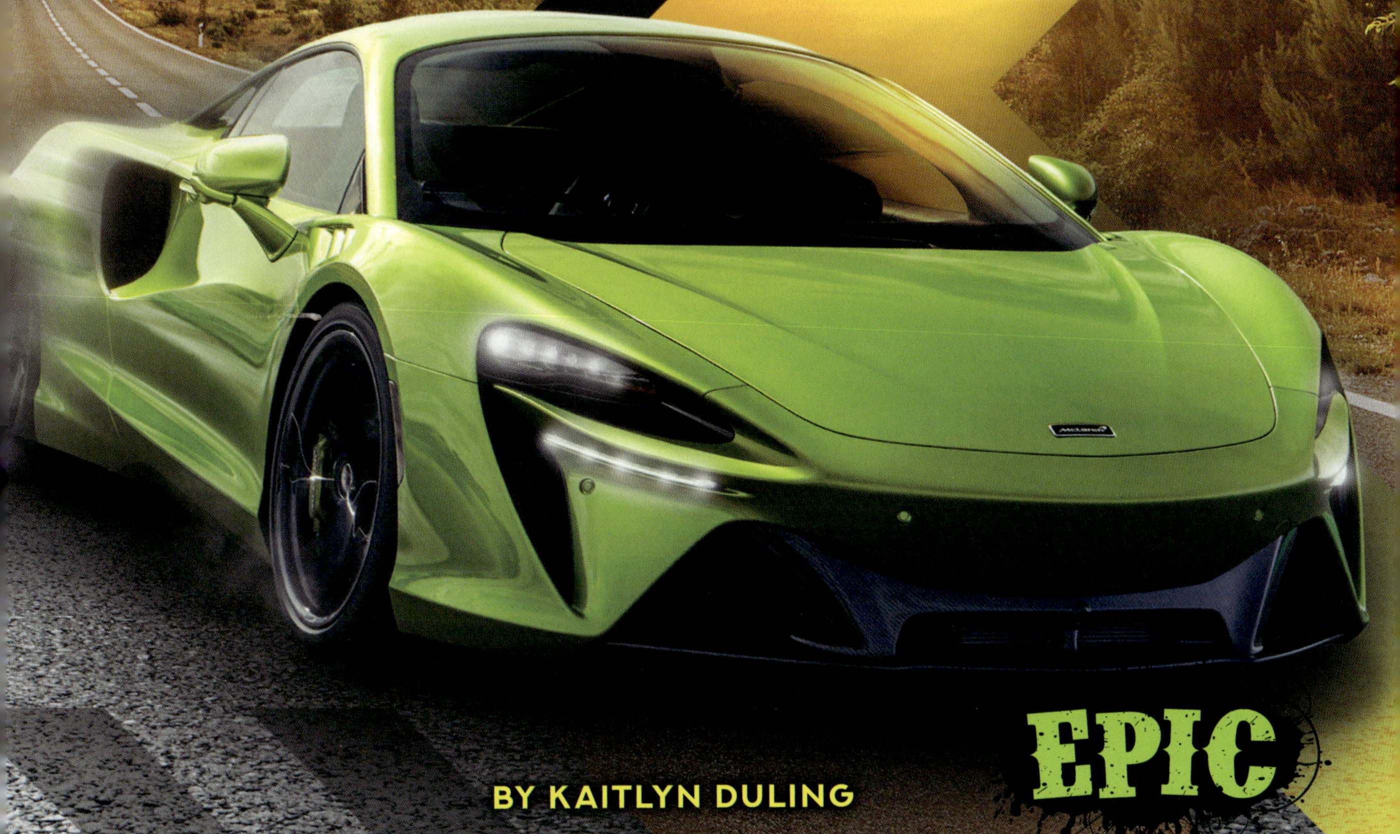

BY KAITLYN DULING

EPIC

BELLWETHER MEDIA ››› MINNEAPOLIS, MN

EPIC

EPIC BOOKS are no ordinary books. They burst with intense action, high-speed heroics, and shadows of the unknown. Are you ready for an Epic adventure?

This edition first published in 2025 by Bellwether Media, Inc.

Library of Congress Cataloging-in-Publication Data

LC record for McLaren Artura available at: https://lccn.loc.gov/2024002294

Editor: Rachael Barnes Designer: Jeffrey Kollock

Printed in the United States of America, North Mankato, MN.

TABLE OF CONTENTS

SNEAKY SPEEDSTER

This **hybrid** car is quiet at first. It gets louder as it speeds down the street!

NAME GAME

The name Artura comes from the words "art" and "future." In 2023, artist Cevin Parker made a special Artura art car.

ALL ABOUT THE ARTURA

BRUCE McLAREN

Bruce McLaren was a race car driver from New Zealand. In 1963, he started his own company in England.

Today, McLaren builds cars for the road and the racetrack. Many McLaren race cars have set **Formula One** records.

FORMULA ONE RACE

WHERE IS IT MADE?

McLaren makes many **supercars**. They are powerful and fast. The 750S and the P1 are famous **models**.

The Artura was released in 2022. It is one of McLaren's first hybrid supercars.

P1

2022 ARTURA

ARTURA BASICS

YEAR FIRST MADE	2022
COST	starts at $237,500
HOW MANY MADE	currently being made

FEATURES

butterfly doors

buttresses

air intakes

PARTS OF THE ARTURA

The Artura's **V6 engine** is the first engine created by McLaren alone. The car also runs on an **electric motor**. It is powered by a **battery**.

Together, they help this hybrid reach 205 miles (330 kilometers) per hour!

ENGINE SPECS

HYBRID TWIN-TURBO V6 ENGINE AND ELECTRIC MOTOR

TOP SPEED	205 miles (330 kilometers) per hour
0-62 TIME	3.0 seconds
HORSEPOWER	671 hp

SMART TIRES

The Artura has specially made tires. They gather information as the car moves.

McLaren created a new support frame for the Artura. The main part is made of **carbon fiber**. This build makes the car lightweight.

SIZE CHART

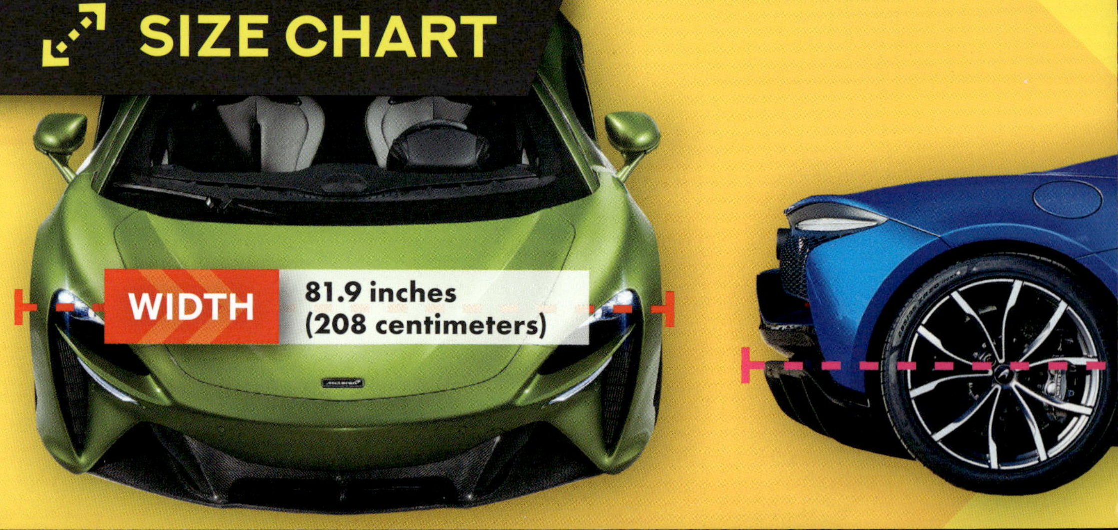

Buttresses and side **air intakes** help air move through the car.

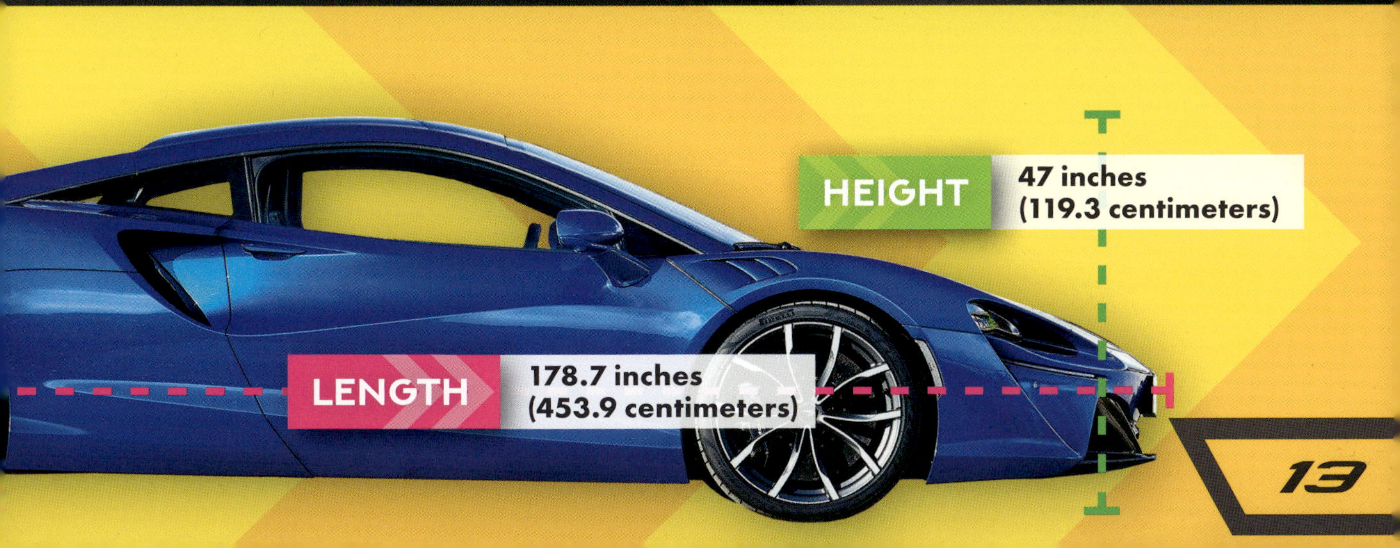

Inside, the Artura has a simple look. Its two seats sit low to the ground.

The Artura has multicolored lighting. Drivers can control the color through a large **touch screen**.

HEAT RELEASE

The Artura has a chimney! There is a special opening near the middle of the car. It lets hot air out from around the engine.

Several features keep drivers safe. The Artura can alert drivers to stop signs and speed signs.

The car's nose can lift up. The driver touches a button. This helps the car drive over bumps.

McLaren added new Artura options in 2023. They honored the company's 60th birthday. New paint colors help owners **customize** their supercar.

60TH BIRTHDAY OPTION

ARTURA GT4

McLaren also added a new track-only model. The Artura GT4 is gas-powered and ready to race!

THE ARTURA'S FUTURE

McLaren will keep making the Artura and other supercars. Many will be hybrids. Others will run on electric motors.

The company plans to build even more powerful cars. They will speed McLaren into the future!

GLOSSARY

air intakes—openings on a car that allow air to reach its engine

battery—a part that supplies electric energy to a car

butterfly doors—car doors that open up and out like butterfly wings

buttresses—parts on a car that add support and direct air around it

carbon fiber—a strong, lightweight material used to strengthen things

customize—to make to personal order

electric motor—a machine that gives something the power to move by using electricity

Formula One—a type of car racing

hybrid—related to a car that uses both a gasoline engine and an electric motor for power

models—specific kinds of cars

supercars—expensive and high-performing sports cars

touch screen—a display on which people can select options by touching the screen

V6 engine—an engine made with 6 cylinders arranged in the shape of a "V"

TO LEARN MORE

AT THE LIBRARY

Adamson, Thomas K. *McLaren 720S.* Minneapolis, Minn.: Bellwether Media, 2023.

Colson, Rob. *Supercars.* New York, N.Y.: Crabtree Publishing, 2022.

Duling, Kaitlyn. *McLaren Elva.* Minneapolis, Minn.: Bellwether Media, 2024.

ON THE WEB

FACTSURFER

Factsurfer.com gives you a safe, fun way to find more information.

1. Go to www.factsurfer.com.
2. Enter "McLaren Artura" into the search box and click 🔍.
3. Select your book cover to see a list of related content.

INDEX

The images in this book are reproduced through the courtesy of: McLaren, front cover, pp. 3, 4, 5, 6 (Bruce McLaren), 8 (main and P1), 9 (isolated, intake, and doors), 10, 11, 12 (main and width), 13 (main, intake, and length), 14 (main and window), 15 (main and touch screen), 16, 17, 18 (60th), 19, 20, 21; Motoring Picture Library/ Alamy, p. 6; Jay Hirano Photography, p. 7; Gabo_Arts, p. 9 (buttresses); DPPI Media/ Alamy; p. 18.